Benigno Núñez Novo

The Brazilian education system

The right to education in Brazil

ScienciaScripts

Imprint

Any brand names and product names mentioned in this book are subject to trademark, brand or patent protection and are trademarks or registered trademarks of their respective holders. The use of brand names, product names, common names, trade names, product descriptions etc. even without a particular marking in this work is in no way to be construed to mean that such names may be regarded as unrestricted in respect of trademark and brand protection legislation and could thus be used by anyone.

Cover image: www.ingimage.com

This book is a translation from the original published under ISBN 978-613-9-62217-7.

Publisher:
Sciencia Scripts
is a trademark of
Dodo Books Indian Ocean Ltd. and OmniScriptum S.R.L publishing group

120 High Road, East Finchley, London, N2 9ED, United Kingdom
Str. Armeneasca 28/1, office 1, Chisinau MD-2012, Republic of Moldova, Europe

ISBN: 978-620-7-27466-6

First of all to God for the willingness to do this work.

Finally, I would like to pay tribute to the friends I have made over the course of this work and to everyone who has contributed to its completion.

SUMMARY

INTRODUCTION

The right to education is part of a set of rights called social rights, which are inspired by the value of equality between people. In Brazil, this right was only recognized in the Federal Constitution of 1988. Before then, the state had no formal obligation to guarantee quality education for all Brazilians. Within the list of fundamental human rights is the right to education, supported by national and international standards. It is a fundamental right because it includes a process of individual development that is proper to the human condition.

Among the list of fundamental

human rights is the right to education, supported by national and international standards. It is a fundamental right, because it includes a process of individual development that is proper to the human condition. Beyond this individual perspective, this right must be seen, above all, collectively, as a right to an educational policy, to affirmative support from the state that offers society the tools to achieve its goals.

The Government, as one of those responsible for promoting education,

must promote support not only in the field of public policy-making (executive), in the field of law-making (legislative), but also in the field of public policy-making (executive), but also in the field of public policy-making (legislative). exercising the role of protector and monitor of this right (judiciary).

The various institutions of public power play important roles in guaranteeing citizens' rights. In a country marked by inequalities such as Brazil, where the distribution of rights mirrors this inequality, guaranteeing the right to education is undoubtedly a priority and a fundamental step towards consolidating citizenship. Education is a common competence of all the federal entities that make up the Brazilian state. It is a subjective public right for all.

Part One

WORLD BANK NOVEMBER 2017 REPORT WITH BRAZILIAN EDUCATION DATA

CHAPTER I

A FAIR ADJUSTMENT: ANALYZING THE EFFICIENCY AND EQUITY OF PUBLIC SPENDING IN BRAZIL

The World Bank report "A Fair Adjustment: Analysis of the efficiency and equity of public spending in Brazil", dated November 21, 2017, on pages 121 to 138, deals with education in Brazil.

Rising public spending and falling public enrollment numbers result in higher spending per student and inefficient student-teacher ratios. For wealthier municipalities, efficiency is even lower given the faster demographic transition, which results in a faster reduction in the number of students in the public school system. The constitutional obligation to spend 25 percent of tax revenues on education contributes to these municipalities increasing their spending per pupil at a faster rate. This additional spending doesn't always translate into greater learning, which leads to inefficiencies. In addition to a relatively low student-teacher ratio, the public education system in Brazil is characterized by low teacher quality and high failure rates. All these factors lead to significant inefficiencies. If all municipalities and states were able to emulate the most efficient school networks, it would be possible to improve performance (in terms of pass rates and student achievement) by 40% in primary education and 18% in secondary education, while maintaining the same level of public spending. Instead, Brazil is spending 62% more than it would need to achieve the performance currently observed in public schools, which corresponds to almost 1% of GDP. Public spending on higher education is also highly inefficient, and almost 50% of resources could be saved. Public spending on primary and secondary education is progressive, but spending on higher education is highly regressive. This indicates the need to introduce tuition fees at universities and to better target access to student financing for higher education (FIES program).

CHAPTER II

EDUCATION SPENDING IN BRAZIL

Public spending on education is divided between the three levels of government. Most of the federal government's spending goes to higher education. In Brazil, municipalities are responsible for the majority of primary schools (1st to 9th grade), while responsibility for secondary education lies with the states. However, the federal government transfers resources to sub-national education systems through budgetary transfers. The federal government also funds public universities and technical and vocational education and training programs. A growing share of federal spending on education is linked to financial assistance offered to students attending private higher education institutions.

Public spending on education has been growing rapidly in recent years, above the levels seen in peer countries. In 2014, after a decade of rapid growth, spending on education reached 6% of GDP. In 2010, spending on education in Brazil was higher than the average for OECD countries (5.5%), BRICS countries (5.1%) and Latin America (4.6%). Public spending on all levels of education increased at a real rate of 5.3% per year between 2000 and 2014.

Spending growth occurred in all areas, but early childhood education and secondary education saw the highest growth rates. Spending per pupil grew even faster (10.1% per year in real terms), as the number of students in public primary and secondary schools fell in the 2000s due to demographic changes and migration to private institutes. In relation to GDP per capita, spending per pupil on primary education almost doubled, from 11.9% of GDP per capita in 2002 to 21.8% in 2014.

Spending on higher education has increased rapidly over the last decade. Enrollment in higher education has tripled in Brazil in the last 15 years, and private institutes have played a key role in this process. Public universities account for 25% of enrollments, with federal universities accounting for 15%

of the total. In 2015, the federal government spent

approximately 0.7% of GDP on higher education, mainly through transfers to federal universities and student loans (through the FIES program, in particular).

The public funds allocated to Brazil's 63 federal universities amounted to around 0.5% of GDP in 2015. Since 2010, the federal budget allocated to federal universities has seen an average annual growth of 12% in nominal terms, or 7% in real terms. Considering the 2% annual growth in enrollment, this represents a real annual increase of 5% in spending per student at federal universities.

Average spending per student in

higher education is not high, but it is considerably higher in the

universities and federal institutes. In 2012, spending per student on higher education was approximately 38% of the average for OECD countries, which is slightly above comparable countries in regional and structural terms. The level of spending per student is comparable to other countries by controlling for GDP per capita. If we consider only public institutes, however, the level of spending per student is close to that seen in countries that have twice the GDP per capita of Brazil, and much higher than that of several OECD countries, such as Italy and Spain. What's more, students at Brazilian public universities on average cost two to three times more than students enrolled in private universities. Despite this much higher cost per student, on average the added value of public universities is similar to the added value of private universities.

CHAPTER III

THE REALITY OF EDUCATION IN BRAZIL

Education results have improved in Brazil, but remain low when you consider the dramatic increase in spending. Despite significant advances in access, completion and learning in the Brazilian education system over the last two decades, the quality of teaching is still very low. Brazil made significant improvements in the PISA (Program for International Student Assessment) math test. Brazil's average score went from 68% to 79% of the OECD average between 2002 and 2012. However, since then, results have fallen to 77% in

2015 (the same level as in 2009). When controlling for the level of spending per student, the PISA results are still disappointing. Brazil's performance as measured by the PISA math test in 2012 was only 83% of that expected for countries with the same level of spending per student. Countries like Colombia and Indonesia, for example, achieved similar PISA scores by spending much less per pupil. Countries like Chile, Mexico and Turkey spend similar amounts to Brazil and achieve better results.

The inefficiency of spending on basic education in Brazil is high and increasing. A Data Envelopment Analysis (DEA) with OECD PISA data on education in Brazil and other Latin

American countries shows that Brazilian schools are relatively inefficient in their use of resources (input-oriented DEA). Furthermore, the average inefficiency increased from around 45% in 2006 to 55% in 2012. Although spending per pupil has increased, most schools have failed to improve performance, resulting in lower overall productivity. Efficiency and performance are correlated: the schools with the best results are also the most efficient. The 25% of schools with the best performance are, on average, 20% more efficient than schools in the second quartile. Although the factors that cause better school performance are largely idiosyncratic and related to school management, larger schools, urban schools and private schools tend to have better performance and efficiency results.

The poor performance of the Brazilian education system is reflected in the high failure and dropout rates, despite the low and decreasing student-teacher ratios. More than 35% of students repeated at least one year in primary and secondary school, compared to less than 15% in the OECD and structurally comparable countries such as Turkey and Russia. Dropout rates are also extremely high (26%) compared to the OECD (4%) and comparable countries in the region (14%). This is despite the fact that Brazil has a relatively low pupil-teacher ratio. In fact, the average student-teacher ratio has been decreasing because the population of students in public education is falling. In 2014, the pupil-teacher ratio was 23 in elementary school, and 19 in elementary school. These figures are above the OECD average (15 and 13, respectively), but slightly below the average for structurally comparable countries (25 and 22 for primary and secondary education, respectively) (OECD, 2014).

The low rate of high school graduation is another indicator of the low performance of the education system. Students graduate from high school at the age of 19 on average, which is slightly above the average of comparable regional and structural countries. However, the high failure and dropout rates observed in Brazil result in a high percentage of students completing high school.

surprisingly high number of students who don't finish high school before the age of 25. This seems to be the main cause of the high costs per high school graduate in Brazil, which are much higher than in any other country in Latin America.

The high educational gap starts in elementary school and continues through to higher education, resulting in a high average cost to educate a student. Brazil has a gross enrollment rate in higher education of 42%, much higher than the corresponding net rate of 16%. This means that more than half of Brazil's higher education students should have graduated by now. Failures are not only costly, but also reflect a lack of support for poorer performing students - often from disadvantaged families.

The low quality of teachers is the main factor restricting
quality of education. Teaching has remained a profession
discredited. The entry requirements for degree courses are weak and the training is of poor quality. In addition to the lack of selectivity in hiring teachers for state and municipal education systems, salaries are not linked to performance. Changing this paradigm will require coordinated public policy reforms at the federal, state and municipal levels. Demographic trends, however, will offer a great opportunity to

raise the level of teachers and the quality of education over the next decade, as it is estimated that the school-age population will decrease by 25% between 2010 and 2025. This, combined with the large number of teachers who will be retiring in the next few years, will allow for greater selection in the hiring of a smaller number of teachers who will be needed to replace those who will be retiring.

The salary floor for Brazilian teachers is in line with what is paid in other countries with a similar per capita income. However, teachers' salaries in Brazil increase rapidly after the start of their careers. Due to automatic promotions based on years of service and participation in training programs, within 15 years of a teacher's career, they are paid more than the average salary.

salaries become two to three times higher than the starting salary, in real terms.

significantly than most countries in the world. In addition, it is worth noting that Brazilian teachers are entitled to relatively generous pension plans when compared to other OECD countries. This generosity of pension benefits is much higher than international standards. While primary school teachers' salaries are in line with countries with similar incomes, university teachers' salaries appear to be more generous than those of other countries.

to be above several countries with a

higher per capita income.

A comparison of the performance of various Brazilian municipalities indicates the possibility of savings equivalent to 1% of GDP if all municipalities emulated those on the performance frontier. The high variation in performance between municipalities partly reflects Brazil's diversity, but also signals the existence of significant inefficiencies. A DEA analysis was carried out comparing performance based on Basic Education Development Index (IDEB) scores and education spending at municipal and state level. On average, the variation in municipal and state spending only explains 11% of IDEB performance, which indicates that Good management practices have an important impact on results. If all schools could match the most efficient ones, performance would improve by 40% in primary education and 18% in secondary education. Instead, Brazil spends 62% more than is necessary for the observed performance.

corresponds to R$56 billion (or almost 1% of GDP). Of this total, R$27 billion and R$15 billion could be saved, respectively, in municipal and state primary education, and R$15 billion in state secondary education.

There is scope for improving performance by increasing spending in the North and Northeast, while the scope for savings is greater in the South, Southeast and Center-West regions. Municipalities and states in the

North and Northeast tend to be more efficient, and additional resources would have a greater impact in these regions. In fact, reducing spending in these regions could negatively affect performance. For schools in states and municipalities in the South, Southeast and Center-West regions that spend more per pupil, reducing spending does not seem to jeopardize results. They tend to be less efficient and could benefit more from improvements in management.

The inefficiency of primary and secondary education is mainly related to the excessive number of teachers. Approximately 39% of the inefficiency of Brazilian spending on education is associated with low student-teacher ratios (PTR). If all schools reached the performance threshold, Brazil could increase the number of students per teacher by 33% in primary education and 41% in secondary education. Alternatively, reducing the number of teachers based on the current number of students would represent a saving of approximately R$ 22 billion (or 0.33% of GDP), of which R$ 17 billion in primary education, and R$ 5 billion in secondary education. Low student-teacher ratios are a significant problem in primary education in the South, Southeast and Center-West regions, where demographic changes are causing the number of students in public schools to fall rapidly. To a large extent, this problem could be solved by not replacing some of the teachers who will soon be retiring. Reducing the number of teachers through retirement could adjust the ratios to efficient levels in primary education by 2027 and in secondary education by 2026.

It is also possible to increase efficiency by making the teachers devote more time to classroom activities and reduce absenteeism. Teachers in Brazil spend a lot of their time on unproductive activities. On average, teachers use only 65% of their time to teach, while according to best practice
The ideal would be 85%. It is also necessary to reduce absenteeism among teachers. In Sao Paulo, for example, the rate is 16% and in

Pernambuco 10% (compared to 5% in the USA). Absences are related to environmental factors (traffic, violence, heat, stress), but are also caused by permissive laws that grant leave for many unverifiable reasons. In addition, disconnects between performance, tenure and pay, and weak monitoring and control mechanisms mean that teachers have little incentive to maintain adequate attendance. International literature offers some possible solutions: introducing an attendance bonus for teachers; improving mechanisms for recording absences and attendance; introducing and enforcing dismissal threats for excessive absenteeism; introducing retirement benefits; and publishing average absenteeism rates in school performance reports.

The constitutional binding of education spending to 25 percent of municipal revenues also contributes to inefficient spending. Wealthier municipalities, with high rates of net current revenue per pupil, tend to be much less efficient than poorer municipalities. Therefore, it is likely that in order to comply with constitutional rules, many wealthy municipalities will be forced to spend on items that do not necessarily enhance learning. This is all the more worrying given the drastic demographic transition the country is going through. With the fertility rate rapidly falling below 1.8, the number of pupils is falling rapidly in many municipalities, especially in elementary school. Given that this drop in pupil numbers is not necessarily associated with a drop in net current revenue, this implies that in order to comply with the law, many municipalities are forced to spend more and more per pupil, even when revenue remains constant. Moreover, this additional spending is often not necessary and therefore does not result in greater learning. The consequence is an even greater increase in inefficiency.

Part Two

POSITIVE EXPERIENCES AND
HIGHER EDUCATION

CHAPTER I

POSITIVE EXPERIENCES

There is no shortage of positive and innovative experiences in Brazil on how to improve the quality of education with limited resources. Innovations in school management in the state of Ceara have shown how to improve significantly improve learning outcomes through performance incentives. In Ceara, the distribution of state tax revenue (the ICMS) is based on each municipality's education quality index. Ceara has also made interventions in student learning, such as the Literacy at an Early Age Program (Programa de Alfabetizapao na Idade).

Certa (PAIC) and introduced the supply of pre-prepared teaching and literacy materials to teachers. In Amazonas, teachers are evaluated shortly after they are hired, and only the best are retained. A compulsory two-hour online course and a final assessment are requirements for all teachers during their probationary period. The states of Rio de Janeiro and Pernambuco have introduced a bonus for teachers and staff based on school performance. Rio de Janeiro also eliminated the political appointment of regional coordinators and school directors, as well as introducing an evaluation of performance for school and regional directors, and regular meetings to disseminate the results and highlight the best-performing schools. All these experiments have proved to be cost-effective, not only improving student performance, but also increasing the efficiency of public spending on education.

CHAPTER II

HIGHER EDUCATION IN BRAZIL

The vast majority of Brazilians enrolled in higher education study at private universities. In 2015, of the approximately 8 million university students, only around two million were at public universities. The small minority of students attending public universities in Brazil tend to be from wealthier families who attended private primary and secondary schools. Even so, spending per student at public universities in Brazil is considerably higher than in other countries with a similar GDP per capita.

On average, a student at public

universities in Brazil costs two to three times more than students at private universities. Between 2013 and 2015, the average annual cost per student at private non-profit and for-profit universities was approximately R$12,600 and R$14,850, respectively. federal universities, the average was R$40,900. State public universities cost less than federal ones, but are still much more expensive than private ones, costing approximately R$32,200. The cost per student at federal institutes, most of which were founded in 2008, is approximately R$27,850.

As students of While public universities tend to perform better in standardized exams, the added value of private universities seems to be similar to that of private universities. The average ENADE score for public universities is higher than for private universities. However, students who enter public universities tend to have already achieved a higher level of learning before they even start their studies. For this reason, the most relevant metric for measuring added value is to compare the score obtained with the pre-university expected score. For exact science courses, private universities tend to add as much value as public universities. For humanities subjects, private universities seem to add more value, except for the Federal Institutes. For the biological sciences, Federal Institutes and state universities add the most value; and federal universities add around the same value per student as private non-profit universities, however, they cost around three times as much.

Private universities Brazilian companies tend to be more cost-effective than public ones. One DEA analysis comparing the cost per student with the ENADE value added index estimates that public universities are on average only 79% cost efficient. In other words, it would be possible to achieve the same performance with around 20% fewer resources. Non-profit and for-profit private universities have an average efficiency of 88% and 86%, respectively.

Estimates indicate that by becoming more efficient, federal universities and institutes could save approximately R$10.5 billion a year and still add the same amount as they do today. State universities could save around R$ 2.7 billion a year.

Public spending on primary and secondary education benefits the poor more than the rich. As the poor depend more on the public school network, public spending on primary education, in particular, is progressive. More than 60% of spending on primary education benefits the bottom 40% of the income distribution. Public spending on primary education II, secondary education and pre-school education is also progressive, although a little less so, as the poorest have less access to these services. In this case, the poorest 40%

benefit from around 50% of total spending.

However, spending on higher education is very regressive. Public higher education receives the lion's share of funding per student (approximately US$5,000 in PPC). Although enrollment in higher education has been rising rapidly in Brazil, access to this level of education remains highly inequitable. In 2002, no university student was among the poorest 20% of the population and only 4% were among the poorest 40%. In 2015, approximately 15% of higher education students were in the 40% poorest group. Public spending on higher education mostly benefits students from wealthier families. In particular, federal universities are fully funded by the federal government and do not charge for tuition. However, only 20% of students are from the poorest 40% of the population, while 65% are from the richest 40%. This injustice is exacerbated by the fact that access to public universities is governed by a very competitive entrance exam. Students from wealthier families can afford to pay for private tutors or attend primary and secondary schools in private schools, which offer better preparation for these entrance exams. Students from poorer families, on the other hand, have much less chance of getting into public universities.

CHAPTER III

THE OECD 2017 REPORT
ON HIGHER EDUCATION IN
BRAZIL

The Organization for Economic Cooperation and Development (OECD) is an international organization of 35 countries that accept the principles of representative democracy and free market economics, which seeks to provide a platform for comparing economic policies, solving common problems and coordinating domestic and international policies. Most OECD members are economies with a high GDP per capita and Human Development Index and are considered developed countries.

It originated in 1948 as the Organization for Economic Cooperation (OECE), led by Robert Marjolin of France, to help manage the Marshall Plan for the reconstruction of Europe after the Second World War. Later, its membership was extended to non-European states. In 1961, the Convention on the Organization for Economic Cooperation and Development reformed the OECE and gave rise to the Organization for Economic Cooperation and Development.
Economical.

The headquarters of the OECD are located at the Chateau de la Muette in Paris, France.

The OECD's 2017 "Education at a Glance" report provides an opportunity to reflect on the challenges facing higher education in Brazil.

The first is to understand the mission of higher education. In Brazil, it is mainly an instrument for professional training. The model may have been suitable for the first half of the 20th century, but it no longer corresponds to advances in economies and technologies.

The trend in more advanced countries is to divide higher education into two parts. The first is general education, where people learn to think in depth.

The stricter they are, the more

"generalist" and less applied, the more important these courses become in a society where we don't know what the jobs of the future will be like. It should be noted that a small part of higher education in developed countries is geared towards the training of technologists, in short courses. The second part of higher education is where students seek higher-level professional training or prepare to start an academic career.

In Brazil, as the professions are hyper-regulated, the curricula are "tied down", with a multitude of subjects and compulsory courses. In other words, quantity is favored over quality. In this respect, we are going against the most advanced countries.

The second challenge is quality. In most developed countries, around 30% of high school graduates go on to higher education, and this figure has been rising over the last few decades. In very few countries, such as the United States, this figure is higher than 50%. In most European countries, access to higher education is still quite restricted and selective, and the institutes - which are almost always public - generally maintain very similar standards.

In Brazil, we have different realities - some universities and courses are selective, but the vast majority are not. According to Pisa data, less than 10% of Brazilian students would be able to access a higher education course in European countries and much less than

1% would be able to compete in elite North American universities. The ENEM data also confirms this situation. In other words, the challenge of quality higher education will only begin to be resolved when the country produces high school graduates with an adequate level of learning.

The third challenge is institutional. The legal framework for higher education in Brazil
and is based on the idea of   of a
a "University of Teaching, Research and Extension", a model initially
implemented in Germany in the 19th century. Not all
Higher education institutions carry out these three activities, which creates an extraordinary cost in order to comply

with the model - or to circumvent the legislation. The management system of public universities does not provide incentives for them to be efficient. The management of private institutes is subject to an extremely costly regulatory tangle that does nothing to increase competition, reduce costs or improve quality. We have huge entry barriers for foreign teachers, reducing the pressure on our own. And we offer very few attractions for good graduate students from other countries.

Part Three

DIAGNOSIS OF HIGHER EDUCATION IN BRAZIL BY THE OECD REPORT 2017

CHAPTER I

THE REALITY OF HIGHER DUCATION ACCORDING TO THE OECD REPORT 2017

The OECD's 2017 "Education at a Glance" Report makes available a study that analyzed the education systems of 45 countries. The study describes that Brazil invests in university students more than three times as much as it spends on primary and secondary school students.

Brazil is one of the countries that spends the least on primary and secondary school pupils, but spending on university students is increasing.

similar to those of European countries, according to the Organization for Cooperation and Development Economy (OECD).

In the study "A Look at Education", the organization analyzes the education systems of the 35 member countries of the organization, the vast majority of which are developed, and ten other economies, such as Brazil, Argentina, China and South Africa.

The Report exposes the contradictions of education in Brazil: half of adult Brazilians do not complete secondary education and teachers' salaries remain low. One of the most striking figures was the information that, in 2015, more than half of adults aged between 25 and 64 did not complete secondary education - another 17% did not complete primary education. These figures are below the average observed in the other countries analyzed by the OECD, in which 22% of adults did not reach secondary school and 2% completed the stages of elementary school.

Another advance observed, on the other hand, was the increase in the percentage of adults (25 to 34 years old) who completed the last stage of basic education from 53% in 2010 to 64% in 2015.

Brazil spends US$3.8 thousand (R$11 .7 thousand) a year per student of the
[a]first cycle of primary education (up to grade 5), the document states. The

dollar value is calculated based on the Purchasing Power Parity (PPP) for international comparison.

The figure represents less than half the average amount spent per year on each student at this stage of school in OECD countries, which is 8.7 thousand dollars. Luxembourg, top of the list, spends 21.2 thousand dollars.

Among the countries analyzed in the study, only six spend less on ten-year-olds than Brazil, including Argentina (US$ 3.4 thousand), Mexico (US$ 2.9 thousand) and Colombia (US$ 2.5 thousand). Indonesia is the country at the bottom, spending just 1.5 thousand dollars.

The situation is no different in the

final years of primary and secondary education. Brazil spends the same amount of US$3,800 per pupil in these cycles every year and is also among the last on the list of the 39 countries that have provided data on the subject.

The average in OECD countries in the final years of primary and secondary education is US$ 10,500 per pupil, which is 176% more than in Brazil.

Only 15% of Brazilian students aged between 25 and 34 are in higher education, compared to 37% in the OECD, 21% in Argentina and 22% in Chile and Colombia. However, compared to the BRICS countries (a bloc made up of Brazil, Russia, India, China and South Africa), Brazil is better off - China has 10%, India 11% and

South Africa 12%.

In Brazil, around 37% of undergraduate degrees in 2015 were in the areas of business, administration and law, a rate similar to most of the other countries surveyed.

Next, the preference of Brazilians at the time was for pedagogy, with 20% of enrollments - one of the highest rates among all countries. The report also shows that only Costa Rica and Indonesia have higher rates of choice for pedagogy (22% and 28%) , respectively).

Only 15% of students Brazilians opted for science, technology, engineering and mathematics, one of the lowest rates, but similar to neighboring countries such as Argentina (14%) and Colombia (13%). Among OECD countries, the percentage was 23%.

In terms of inequality in access to higher education, in Brazil the disparity between the states is the greatest observed in the survey. While 35% of young people aged 25 to 34 in the Federal District attend university, in Maranhao the rate is five times lower (7%).

Although the report recognizes that Brazil is a very large and diverse nation, compared to other large ones such as the United States and Russia, inequality is much more dramatic here, with variations of up to five times in the percentages, compared to less than three times in other countries.

A counterpoint to this, however, is that almost 75% of Brazilian students in higher education are in private institutions, compared to around 33% on average in OECD countries.

The report warns, however, that in this case, the lack of student financing mechanisms can be an obstacle and programs like Fies may have helped put Brazilians through college here.

The situation in Brazil changes when it comes to spending on university students: the amount rises to almost US$11,700 (R$36,000), more than three times the amount spent on primary and secondary education.

With this amount, Brazil is close to

some European countries, such as Portugal, Estonia and Spain, with expenditure per university student of US$ 11.8 thousand, US$ 12.3 thousand and US$ 12.5 thousand respectively, and even surpasses countries such as Italy (US$ 11.5 thousand), the Czech Republic (US$ 10.5 thousand) or Poland (US$ 9.7 thousand).

The average in OECD countries is US$ 16,100, driven by higher spending in countries such as the United States, Norway, Luxembourg and the United Kingdom.

Spending on university students in Brazil also exceeds that of South Korea, at U$ 9.6 thousand.

The Asian country, which spends

a little more on primary education (U$ 9,700), is among the top performers in the OECD's Program for International Student Assessment (PISA). The test measures 15-year-old students' knowledge of science, mathematics and reading comprehension.

Brazil, on the other hand, is among the last countries in the PISA test and only 17% of young people aged between 25 and 34 have a university degree, one of the lowest rates among the countries in the study.

On average, OECD members spend almost half as much per university student as they do on primary students, says the document, "while Brazil and Mexico spend three times as much".

The OECD has highlighted in recent studies that there has been an increase in public investment in education in Brazil. As a percentage of GDP, Brazil is close to the average of the organization's countries.

Spending on education amounted to 4.9% of Brazil's GDP (the last figure available in the study). The average for OECD countries is 5.2% of GDP.

At the same time, the OECD has been saying that it is necessary to increase spending per pupil in primary and secondary education, which is well below the amount considered adequate by the organization.

Despite the improvement in the level of investment in education in

Brazil, Brazil still ranks among the bottom in the PISA assessment tests.

In the organization's assessment, this is because there has been greater access to education in the country, with the inclusion of disadvantaged students and those with learning delays in the education system, which ends up pulling down the overall performance of Brazilian students.

CHAPTER II

THE CHALLENGES OF EDUCATION IN BRAZIL

It is possible to save almost 1% of GDP by improving efficiency in primary and secondary education, without compromising the current level of services provided. Some reform options to increase efficiency at these levels of education. Allowing the pupil-teacher ratio to increase in the most inefficient schools in order to gradually reach efficiency levels by not replacing retiring teachers. On average, the efficiency frontier would be reached in primary education by 2027 if retiring teachers were not replaced; in secondary education, the frontier would be reached by 2026. This measure alone would save up to 0.33% of GDP. Another recommendation for municipalities that need to replace retiring teachers would be to limit the hiring of new teachers, whose dismissal is extremely difficult and whose costs are significant, since they retire early with full salaries. Expand and share positive school management experiences that have shown good results in various states and municipalities across the country. Some good examples of interventions that could be replicated are: appointing school directors based on their performance and experience (rather than political appointments); paying bonuses to teachers and staff based on school performance; adapting state policies to specific local needs; sharing experiences and best practices; and highlighting the best performing schools.

Brazil faces huge challenges in getting its higher education right. There are islands of excellence here and there - but they are islands in which institutions, professors and researchers pay a high price to avoid succumbing to generalized mediocrity .

he progress of a nation depends largely on the quantity and quality of its elites, and this is directly related to the quality of higher education. Public education in Brazil must remain free and of high quality for students who cannot afford it, as a matter of social justice.

Adults with a university education

are also less likely to suffer from depression than those who have not reached higher education. Young adults are increasingly willing to get an education in Brazil that increases their skills, rather than entering the job market directly after completing compulsory education. Between 2000 and 2016, the percentage of young people aged 20 to 24 who continued studying increased by 10%, compared to a decrease of 9% for those who were working.

Bibliographical references

1.   BRAZIL. Political Constitution of the Empire of Brazil, of March 25, 1824. Rio de Janeiro, 1824.

2.   BRAZIL. Law of October 15, 1827. Orders the creation of primary schools in all the cities, towns and most populous places in the Empire. Rio de Janeiro, 1827.

3.   ARANHA, Maria Lucia de Arruda. History of Education and Pedagogy. 3rd ed. Sao Paulo: Moderna, 2009. p. 222.

4.   BARROSO, Jose Liberato. Public education in Brazil. Rio de Janeiro: Garnier, 1867.

5.   BRAZIL. Law no. 16 of August 12,

1834. Makes some changes and additions to the Political Constitution of the Empire, under the terms of the Law of October 12, 1832. Rio de Janeiro, 1834.

6. DALLABRIDA, N. The Francisco Campos reform and the nationalized modernization of secondary education. Educagao, Porto Alegre, v. 32, n. 2, p. 185-191, May/Aug. 2009.

7. ARANHA, 2009, p. 224-225.

8. BRAZIL. Decree no. 7.247/1879. Reforms primary and secondary education in the municipality of Corte and higher education throughout the Empire. Rio de Janeiro, 1879.

9. PALMA FILHO, Joao Cardoso. Brazilian Educational Policy. Sao Paulo:

CTE, 2005.

10. BRAZIL. Decree No. 981, of November 8, 1890. Approves the Regulations for Primary and Secondary Education in the Federal District. Rio de Janeiro, 1890.

11. BRAZIL. Constitution of Republic of the United States of Brazil, of February 24, 1891. Rio de Janeiro, 1891.

12. BRAZIL. Decree No. 3.890, of January 1, 1901. Approves the Code of the Official Institutes of Higher and Secondary Education, under the Ministry of Justice and Internal Affairs. Rio de Janeiro, 1901.

13. BRAZIL. Decree No. 3.914, of January 23, 1901. Approves the

regulations for the National Gymnasium. Rio de Janeiro, 1901.

14. BRAZIL. Decree No. 8.659, of April 5, 1911. Approves the Organizing Law for Higher and Elementary Education in the Republic. Rio de Janeiro, 1911.

15. BRAZIL. Decree No. 11.530, of March 18, 1915. Reorganizes secondary and higher education in the Republic. Rio de Janeiro, 1915.

16. BRAZIL. Decree No. 16.782-A, of January 13, 1925. Establishes the competition of the Union for the diffusion of primary education, organization National Department of Education, reform of secondary and higher education and other measures. Rio de

Janeiro, 1925.

17.   ARANHA, 2009, p. 302-304.

18.   AZEVEDO, Fernando [et al.]. A reconstrupao educacional no Brasil: ao povo e ao governo; manifesto of the pioneers of Educapao Nova. Sao Paulo: Cia. Editora Nacional, 1932.

19.   BRAZIL. Decree no. 19.890/1931. Provides for the organization of secondary education. Rio de Janeiro, 1931.

20.   BRAZIL. Decree no. 21.241/1932. Consolidates the provisions on the organization of secondary education and makes other provisions. Rio de Janeiro, 1932.

21.   PALMA, 2005, p. 35.

22.   BRAZIL. Decree-Law .

4.073/1942. Lei organica do ensino industrial. Rio de Janeiro, 1942.

23.   BRAZIL. Decree-Law No. 4.244/1942. Leiorganicado education secundario. Rio de Janeiro, 1942.

24.   BRASIL. Decreto-Lein . 6.141/1943. LeiOrganicadoEnsino Commercial. Rio de Janeiro, 1943.

25.   BRASIL. Decreto-Lein . 8.529/1946. LeiOrganicadoEnsino Primario. Rio de Janeiro, 1946.

26.   BRASIL. Decreto-Lein . 8.530/1946. Lei Organica do Ensino Normal. Rio de Janeiro, 1946.

27.   BRASIL. Decreto-Lein . 9.613/1946. Lei Organica do Ensino Agricola. Rio de Janeiro, 1946.

28.   BRASIL. Decreto-Lein .

9.724/1946. Approves the Agreement between the Ministry of Education and Health and the Inter-American Educational Foundation Inc. on vocational industrial education, and makes other provisions. Rio de Janeiro, 1946.

29. OTRANTO, C. R.; PAMPLONA, R. M. Professional Education from Brazil Imperio to the Capanema Reform: dichotomy in Brazilian education and society. In: V Congresso Brasileiro de Historia da Educagao, 2008, Aracaju. Teaching and Research in the History of Education, 2008.

30. BRAZIL. Constitution of the Estados Unidos do Brasil, of September 18, 1946. Rio de Janeiro, 1946.

31.   MARIANI, Clemente. Exposipao de motivos da mensagem presidencial n. 605 de 29 de outubro de 1948. Diario do Congresso Nacional, 13/11/1948, p. 11615-11617.

32.   BRAZIL. Law n. 4.024/1961. Establishes the Guidelines and Bases of National Education. Brasilia, 1961.

33.   HENTSCHKE, JensR . Reconstructing the Brazilian nation. Public schooling in the Vargas era. Baden-Baden: Nomos, 2007 pgs. 136145.

34.   BRAZIL.   Law   5.540/1968. Establishes
 rules of organization and
functioning of higher education and its articulation with the middle school, and

other measures. Brasilia, 1968.

35. BATTISTUS, C.; LIMBERGER, C.; CASTANHA, A. Estado militar e as reformas educacionais. Revista Educere et Educare, Cascavel, v. 1, n. 1, p. 227232, 2006.

36. ROTHEN, Jose Carlos. Behind the scenes of the 1968 university reform. Educ. Soc., Campinas, v. 29, n. 103, p. 453-475, 2008.

37. BRAZIL. Law 5.692/1971. Establishes Guidelines and Bases for 1st and 2nd grade education, and makes other provisions. Brasilia, 1971.

38. ARANHA, 2009, p. 316-318.

39. BRAZIL. Decree no. 68.908/1971. Decree on entrance exams for admission to higher education courses.

Brasilia, 1971.

40. BRAZIL. Law n. 7.044/1982. Amends provisions of Law No. 5.692, of August 11, 1971, relating to the professionalization of secondary education. Brasilia, 1982.

http://documents.worldbank.org/curated
/en/884871511196609355/pdf/121480-
REVISED-PORTUGUESE-Brazil-
Public-Expenditure-Review-Overview-
Portuguese-Final-revised.pdf

http://www.oecd-
ilibrary.org/docserver/download/961704
2e.pdf?expires=1505742573&id=id&acc
name=guest&checksum=9A147370355
3566C867665F6E09222A1

Milton Keynes UK
Ingram Content Group UK Ltd.
UKHW010853280324
440101UK00001B/225